This book is dedicated to my wife, Donna, whose love, devotion, patience and understanding has made our marriage a delight.

CONTENTS

FOREWORD

Your marriage can be filled with comfort, joy, and the excitement of love that grows through the years; or it may be just another divorce statistic. It is your choice.

I was first married while still in college. Like most college juniors, I though I had all the answers necessary for a happy and lasting marriage. I had studied psychology, human relationships and theology. The truth is, I knew little about relationships and the bit of knowledge I possessed was purely academic. My marriage was a disaster.

I moved into marriage too quickly, and for the wrong reasons, in spite of the advice of older and wiser friends. At the time, I could not have sensibly answered Question #1, Chapter 3—Why do you wish to marry this person?

My failed marriage prompted an increased interest in marital relationships and I completed a Master's Degree with studies primarily in psychology and counseling. Later, while working on my Ph.D., I continued studies in psychology and counseling and attended special programs in Neurolinguistics.

Now, my wife, Donna and I have been married twenty-one wonderful years. During that time, not a single argument—no yelling, no hateful stares, no walking out of the room while the other is talking. We strictly follow the Techniques for Communication as outlined in Chapter II and we are both convinced that no one wins an argument.

It is wonderful to wake up each morning, look into Donna's eyes, snuggle a bit, and feel comfortably assured that together we can face anything.

PLANNING YOUR MARRIAGE was written after years as a pre-marital and marriage counselor. The questions and discussion topics are those used in guiding counselees to improved relationships. I am convinced this planning guide will work for you during your engagement or after years of marriage.

It is my hope that your marriage will be as wonderfully fulfilling as Donna and I experience daily. It takes planning, understanding, honesty, unselfishness, and communication. We both wish you happy planning and a glorious marriage experience.

Chapter I

The Engaging Process of Marriage

Engaged couples spend a great amount of time and energy planning their wedding. Usually in the excitement of engagement, very little attention is given to planning the marriage.

It's a natural, acceptable pattern—boy meets girl, (or if you prefer, man meets woman), they date, fall in love, get engaged, set a date, and start planning the wedding. The bride is in a frenzy from the beginning. Perhaps her mental state may best be described by the acronym, PHEW!—Planning Her Exciting (sometimes extravagant) Wedding. She has dreamed of a wedding since childhood, visualizing herself walking down the aisle in the presence of family and friends. Her Day! Finally, the time has come.

There are many questions and much work to be done. Where will the wedding be? What about a wedding coordinator? There is the invitation list, the bridal gown, bridesmaids' dresses, a photographer, flowers, color scheme, reception and catering. PHEW!

There are some things that the groom must do, but few compared to the many tasks of the bride. He must arrange for a tux, name the best man and groomsmen and perhaps make notes for a brief speech at the reception. The honeymoon—where will it be? How much will it cost? How long can we afford to stay? Wow! When he bought the ring, it all seemed so beautifully simple!

In recall, most couples agree that the wedding and accompanying parties and dinners were wonderful, but it all required far too much time, energy, emotion and money. Perhaps that's the reason more couples go to the local courthouse, a justice of the peace, or escape to Las Vegas.

The purpose of *Planning Your Marriage* is to help engaged couples

1

plan beyond the wedding. The greater amount of time, energy and serious conversation should be directed toward the marriage. It is not my intention to diminish the importance of a wedding ceremony. However, as grand or as simple as it may be, the wedding lasts only one day. Marriage is intended for a lifetime.

There are different types and levels of love. During dating and courtship, romantic love is very exciting. However, lasting relationships are built on a greater depth of love and the art of communication and shared feelings, which go far beyond sexual excitement and romance.

During your marriage there will be times when disagreements come, and communication is difficult. Husband and wife will, at times, have strong feelings regarding what may later be interpreted as an insignificant subject, and one or both may be unyielding, even resistant to the opinions of the other. It is at such a time that oneness requires work on the part of both husband and wife.

Communication is the most important ingredient in marriage. Realtors often say that the value of property is related to location, location, location. In marriage, success depends upon communication, communication, communication.

There will be times when *touchy* questions arise—where to go on vacation, how much money to spend on hobbies, how or when to discipline children, the intrusion of in-laws, whether or not to buy a new car, and a wide variety of other things on which you may differ in opinions. Trouble can start as easily as the wife feeling the need for new household appliances at the time the husband desperately wants new power tools for his garage; or the wife may wish to visit family when the husband may feel the need for quiet time. Such differences of opinion may create problems, if there is insufficient communication.

The seventy questions and topics in the following chapters are for the bride and groom to discuss during their engagement period. The topics are intended to help you freely discuss problems that will likely arise later during your marriage. Discussing such potential problems prior to the wedding may help you avoid many pitfalls following the ceremony. In each section, there will be numerous questions, discussion topics, and advice on methodology. Give each one the time it deserves. Later, when problems arise, you will be ready.

Chapter II

Effective Communication

The bride and groom may immediately agree on many of the seventy topics for discussion in the following chapters. Other subjects may require give and take. There may be some matters on which the couple disagrees completely.

When there is a disagreement, give the subject special attention. Disagreements often lead to arguments. Although arguments are common between married couples, and are often worked through and forgotten, they sometimes leave *sore spots* or *touchy areas* which tend to make positive communication a bit difficult.

There will be matters on which bride and groom or husband and wife have different feelings. It is important that each party expresses their feelings without reservation and the other should listen closely and consider those feelings. I suggest the following *Communication Techniques*. These techniques are effective before and after the wedding.

COMMUNICATION TECHNIQUES

1. **Sit down at a table across from each other. Position yourselves so you can look directly in your partner's eyes.**

   Sitting is very important when you are discussing a critical issue, a touchy subject, or something that *bugs* one or both of you. Standing may be interpreted as an aggressive posture and tends to promote louder conversation, even argument.

   While sitting at the table, each of you should have a favorite beverage. Having something in your hands will lessen motions and gestures that may suggest a negative attitude.

2. **Start the conversation by asking your spouse's permission to state your feelings.**

   Either the bride or the groom may speak first. However, it is important that each give the other sufficient time to reply. When one is speaking, the other should listen and <u>never</u> interrupt.

   Let us assume that the bride initiates the conversation. She may say something like this: "Honey, may I tell you how I feel about buying new furniture at this time?" That is, she asks her groom's permission to express her feelings on a subject where she, perhaps, holds a different view or opinion than his.

   The groom, remembering that love is kind, will say, "Sure, honey, tell me how you feel." Then the bride speaks freely but positively, kindly and considerately about how she feels concerning the particular matter at hand. The groom listens. Under no condition should he interrupt.

   When the bride is completely finished, the groom may say, "Honey, I understand your feelings and I appreciate them. Now, may I tell you how I feel about this matter." Obviously, the bride will say, "Yes, you may." And so this process continues. Usually, with discussion and negotiation, the couple reaches agreement and satisfaction, having shared feelings.

3. **Always talk about feelings. Feelings are more important than facts.**

   Feelings are neither right nor wrong. However, feelings are extremely important.

   My wife, Donna, sometimes feels it is cool in our house when I, at the same time, feel it is warm. The room temperature does not change as a result of our feelings. The thermometer reading at the time is insignificant. Neither person is right or wrong. It is a matter of feeling. So, because we appreciate each other's feelings, I may change the temperature setting or Donna will slip on a sweater.

Do not muddy the waters of communication by citing facts or should-have-been-forgotten events. Talk about feelings.

4. **Never speak to your partner in a loud voice.**

Increased volume suggests distance. After all, your mate is sitting just across the table. Soft words can be heard.

Imagine that you were walking downtown and saw a friend across the street. You may choose to yell in a loud voice because of two factors: the distance across the street and/or noise and confusion of traffic. In such a case, to yell would seem appropriate and necessary. But now, back to the conversation at the table—there is not a great distance between you, nor should there be confusion to distract your attention from one another. For one to raise their voice under such conditions would suggest a feeling of psychological distance.

5. **Discuss only the subject at hand. Talk only about the immediate present and the future.**

Both men and women, but primarily the female of the species, when frustrated, wishing to prove a point or perhaps make an accusation, tend to mentally drop back months, even years, recall past events and throw old quotes abruptly into the conversation. Usually such a damaging regression starts by one party saying something like, "Remember when we were at mother's house back in August and you said …" Such a blast out of the past usually puts the other party on the defensive. Then it is easy to violate technique #4—volume. From that point, things can go downhill fast.

Keep it current. Talk about now and the future. The past can never be retrieved. Be sure that your discussions and your sharing of feelings are quiet, respectful and current.

Practice these techniques as you discuss the questions and topics that follow. Although there is reference to bride and groom, these *Communication Techniques* should continue to be used throughout marriage and practiced at any time there is disagreement or a difference of opinion that may lead to anger.

Chapter III

Matters Relating to Relationship

The process of discussing the following questions will improve your relationship before and after the wedding. The bride and the groom should consider each topic individually, perhaps some notes taken for future reference, and then each question should be discussed by the couple. It is important to make notes of the bride/wife and groom/husband's response. Obviously each person should enter their own thoughts on the topic. Negotiations/decision should be agreed upon by the couple and notations made as a reminder for future reference.

At all times, remember your relationship is the most important matter in marriage. If the two of you are truly together in all things, outside pressures will tend to be less problematic. Of course when children come, family relationships will be expanded. However, even then, it is the relationship between the two of you that is of utmost importance.

Remember, when necessary, refer to the *Communication Techniques* in Chapter II.

1. **Why do I wish to marry this person?**

   The response, "because I love him/her," is not an acceptable answer.

   There are many men and women among your acquaintances, perhaps several of them whom you dated previously. Exactly, why do you wish to marry this one?

   Tell your partner the things about him/her that you find attractive— mannerisms, habits, honesty, dependability, positive nature and perhaps even little idiosyncrasies. The very act of verbalizing your attraction will bring you closer as a couple.

   Bride/Wife's Response:

   _____
   _____
   _____
   _____
   _____
   _____
   _____

   Groom/Husband's Response:

   _____
   _____
   _____
   _____
   _____
   _____
   _____

   Negotiations/Decision:

   _____
   _____
   _____
   _____
   _____
   _____
   _____

2. **Am I sufficiently acquainted with my partner's personal history; i.e., family background, education, health, emotional stability, life goals, work ethics, religious beliefs, etc.?**

It is extremely important that bride and groom, individually, consider these critical factors that relate to a lasting and happy relationship. These matters have to do with communication, your sacred space, and long-term comfort.

Each of these subjects, particularly family, emotional stability and religious beliefs, are important to future wellbeing. After all, when you take a spouse, you take the spouse's family also.

Of these several matters, emotional stability may be the most crucial. It is important for both parties to understand that the person they marry will probably be much the same in temperament twenty, thirty or more years from now.

Many brides and grooms go into marriage feeling that they will change things about their partner—habits, mannerisms, viewpoints, etc.—it usually does not happen.

Bride/Wife's Response:

_____
_____
_____
_____
_____
_____

Groom/Husband's Response:

_____
_____
_____
_____
_____
_____

Negotiations/Decision:

_____
_____
_____
_____
_____
_____

3. **Do I feel free to discuss my emotional, sexual needs and expectations with him/her?**

   Many couples have told me that during the dating years they were always "hot to trot." Then, shortly after marriage, one or both became sexually and/or emotionally cool.

   Sexual and emotional problems sometimes result from change. For instance, following the birth of a child, a woman sometimes becomes less interested in sex and is completely immersed in caring for the child. During such times, the husband may feel he has moved from first to second place in his wife's life. Such problems often go unarticulated but are, nevertheless, depressing. Again, the key is communication!

   Both bride and groom need to understand their own expectations of their mate and his/her expectations of them. How will you know without discussion?

   For some unknown reason, many women expect their husbands to read their mind and know their wishes. Husbands don't know. They must be told.

   Bride/Wife's Response:

   _____
   _____
   _____
   _____
   _____
   _____

   Groom/Husband's Response:

   _____
   _____
   _____
   _____
   _____
   _____

   Negotiations/Decision:

   _____
   _____
   _____
   _____
   _____
   _____

4. **Am I willing to make the necessary investment of time and energy to meet my partner's expectations?**

    This is a question that can only be answered individually by the bride and groom. You must each think it through for yourself. First, you must understand your mate's expectations. Only then, will you be able to determine if you are willing to make the necessary life-style changes to meet those expectations. Remember, your mate's expectations of you are not just for the present.

    Again, communication is crucial. Talk about expectations—not with a family member, a fellow employee, or friend—only with each other.

    Bride/Wife's Response:

    _____
    _____
    _____
    _____
    _____
    _____
    _____
    _____

    Groom/Husband's Response:

    _____
    _____
    _____
    _____
    _____
    _____
    _____
    _____

    Negotiations/Decision:

    _____
    _____
    _____
    _____
    _____
    _____
    _____
    _____

5. **Am I convinced that my partner is able and willing to meet my expectations in marriage?**

    I vividly remember one counseling session. The bride was outgoing and conversational to the point of frustration. She liked parties and visiting with friends and relatives. She enjoyed being the belle of the ball. On the other hand, the groom was a good, quiet, and honest man who looked forward to being a husband and father, but he did not enjoy parties or family gatherings. In spite of advice to delay the wedding, the two were married. After a few troublesome years, the marriage ended in divorce. In this case, both the bride and groom expected the other to change. Such adjustments do not usually happen.

    Bride/Wife's Response:

    _____
    _____
    _____
    _____
    _____
    _____
    _____
    _____

    Groom/Husband's Response:

    _____
    _____
    _____
    _____
    _____
    _____
    _____

    Negotiations/Decision:

    _____
    _____
    _____
    _____
    _____
    _____
    _____

6. **Will we negotiate differences in expectations?**

Most engaged couples will answer—sure we will! That, of course, is said before marriage, before children, before bills and other obligations that can be devastating.

Understand your partner's expectations before the ceremony. Decide if you are willing to meet them or at least how you will negotiate. Will you seek counseling? To whom will you go for help? Decide together now on a course of action.

Most importantly, decide if the changes required in your lifestyle, in order to meet your partner's expectations, are greater than you can comfortably and willingly bear. In some cases, there are such differences in expectations that negotiation fails. Better to fail now, before the wedding, than after.

Bride/Wife's Response:

_____
_____
_____
_____
_____
_____
_____
_____

Groom/Husband's Response:

_____
_____
_____
_____
_____
_____

Negotiations/Decision:

_____
_____
_____
_____
_____
_____
_____

7. **Does my partner have habits that annoy me?**

Every person has habits—the way they move their hands, the use of certain words and phrases, playing with their glasses, clearing their throat, or games and hobbies which seem to be unending. Our personal habits are never strange. Other people's habits may be quirky and aggravating.

The habits that your partner has now will probably be the same habits they exhibit near retirement. Talk about them now. The outcome may be one of two: first, you discuss in honest and open communication, and negotiation may bring change; or second, you may agree to live with them quietly and understandingly.

Bride/Wife's Response:

_____
_____
_____
_____
_____
_____
_____
_____

Groom/Husband's Response:

_____
_____
_____
_____
_____
_____
_____
_____

Negotiations/Decision:

_____
_____
_____
_____
_____
_____
_____

8. **Do I feel comfortable sharing my deepest feelings, positive or negative, with my partner?**

   If you don't, and if you do not wish to do so, the marriage probably will fail. Sharing your feelings openly, honestly and completely is the key ingredient to a happy and lasting relationship.

   For many people, sharing of feelings is difficult. Such people are convinced that if they tuck their feelings away, and cover them with activity, they will go away. They do not go away; it will not work. Beyond that, hidden feelings may abruptly surface at the most unlikely times and cause or increase problems.

   Communication Techniques in Chapter II. Sit down comfortably, ask permission to share your feelings, be a respectful listener, and remember love can outlast anything. Love requires effort on your part. Otherwise it may fade.

   Bride/Wife's Response:

   _____
   _____
   _____
   _____
   _____
   _____
   _____

   Groom/Husband's Response:

   _____
   _____
   _____
   _____
   _____
   _____
   _____

   Negotiations/Decision:

   _____
   _____
   _____
   _____
   _____
   _____
   _____

9. **Are there important disagreements between the two of you that never seem to get resolved?**

    Most disagreements can be resolved through communication. Sometimes it requires a great amount of work on the part of both parties. For one party to simply cave, is insufficient, and will not solve the problem. It will rear its ugly head at a later date. If the matter is important to either of you, work out the disagreement now. If not, don't print the invitations. Some couples think that they can agree to disagree. It seldom works. When there is another, even unrelated touchy topic, the former subject of disagreement or feelings related to it tends to slip in and cause additional problems.

    Bride/Wife's Response:

    _____
    _____
    _____
    _____
    _____
    _____
    _____
    _____

    Groom/Husband's Response:

    _____
    _____
    _____
    _____
    _____
    _____
    _____
    _____

    Negotiations/Decision:

    _____
    _____
    _____
    _____
    _____
    _____
    _____
    _____

10. **Are there particular topics that are difficult to discuss—matters that tend to be incendiary?**

In most relationships that evolve toward engagement and marriage, there will, at times, be emotionally charged disagreements. Couples usually identify topics on which they differ intellectually and emotionally. These are often referred to as picky subjects, hot topics, or incendiary and explosive matters. It is wise to recognize early in a relationship that love does not necessarily eradicate differences.

A couple who differs on such crucial matters as politics and religion, or perhaps the method of rearing children, may find communication on those topics to be difficult. In areas such as politics, it is usually possible to disagree successfully. On other subjects, particularly religion, the role of in-laws, and disciplining of children, it is far more difficult. Solve these problems prior to marriage. If you cannot find agreement, negotiate satisfactory settlements. Learn to love each other because of, rather than in spite of, differences.

Bride/Wife's Response:

_____
_____
_____
_____
_____
_____
_____

Groom/Husband's Response:

_____
_____
_____
_____
_____
_____
_____

Negotiations/Decision:

_____
_____
_____
_____
_____
_____

11. **Am I satisfied with the amount of affection I receive from my partner?**

    Most couples find a satisfactory answer to this question during the dating period and engagement. If your partner is not affectionate then, you have a problem. Any matter of perceived lack of affection should be discussed immediately.

    Sit down, follow the techniques for successful communication in Chapter II, and explain to your partner what is missing and how the void may be filled. Perhaps there is a misunderstanding or your partner is suffering some frustration. There could be a medical problem. Men are slow to initiate conversations of this type. Ladies, make sure it happens. I do not think it is trite to say that affection leads to connection, connection brings about conversation and conversation solves problems.

    Bride/Wife's Response:

    _____
    _____
    _____
    _____
    _____
    _____
    _____

    Groom/Husband's Response:

    _____
    _____
    _____
    _____
    _____
    _____
    _____

    Negotiations/Decision:

    _____
    _____
    _____
    _____
    _____
    _____
    _____

12. **Does my partner respect me as a person?**

This simple question is also one of the most complicated. By all means, married couples must respect each other. Slight differences can work as a catalyst to bring them closer. On the other hand, if the lack of respect seems to come about after marriage or after children, there may be a very precise cause. Usually, people who are disrespectful are lacking in self-respect. In the same manner that we are unable to love others until we learn to love ourselves, it is difficult to respect others until we learn self-respect.

The question regarding respect from a partner may be extremely difficult. It could have more to do with perception than actual lack of respect. Sometimes a bride or groom may be a bit on edge, particularly just prior to the marriage. In such cases, it is possible to interpret slight disagreements or hesitancy on the part of your partner to become immediately involved in a particular idea, as a lack of respect for you as a person or perhaps for an opinion that you hold dear.

Bride/Wife's Response:

_____
_____
_____
_____
_____
_____

Groom/Husband's Response:

_____
_____
_____
_____
_____
_____

Negotiations/Decision:

_____
_____
_____
_____
_____
_____

13. **Does my partner appreciate my deepest feelings, needs and ideas?**

Appreciation comes through understanding. Understanding comes by learning. Learning usually comes through hearing, seeing or other personal experiences. If your partner seems to lack appreciation for your feelings, it may be that they do not sufficiently understand your feelings or needs. Be sure to articulate your needs clearly. This process requires time and a clear statement of your personal expectations. Take the time now, before the wedding. Minutes now may save you hours of frustration later in the marriage.

Bride/Wife's Response:

_____

_____

_____

_____

_____

_____

_____

_____

Groom/Husband's Response:

_____

_____

_____

_____

_____

_____

_____

_____

Negotiations/Decision:

_____

_____

_____

_____

_____

_____

_____

14. **Have we spent enough time planning our life together?**

Of course, this is a question only the bride and groom can answer. In most cases, the answer is a resounding NO. There is more than enough planning for the wedding, but very little planning for your life together. But you are doing it now. Congratulations!

CHAPTER IV

Building a Home: Domestic Matters

In order to establish a peaceful home, it is necessary to have early discussions related to your desires—preferred type of residence, living conditions, division of labor around the house, and general expectations regarding standard of living. While these things may seem to be insignificant in the total scheme of marriage, such matters do, in fact, cause major disagreements or result in a general sense of irritation that often magnifies the relative importance of other areas of disagreement in the marriage. For example: if a woman is not thrilled with her employment or the amount of time her husband spends away from home, adding unhappiness related to the place of residence could be a deal breaker. There must be a place to come home to that you feel to be comfortable and peaceful. To assure themselves that such a home is in their future, the following questions should be seriously discussed by the bride and groom prior to marriage and before the purchase of property.

15. **In what geographic area do we wish to reside; i.e., region, state, city, etc.?**

Most of my time in marriage counseling was in Southern California. That area seems to attract many single men and women who move there to find a new and improved lifestyle. Many of them seek employment in the entertainment industry. Consequently, a young man from the upper Midwest may meet a beautiful young lady from New Mexico. They fall in love and are married. The husband has, all the while, had dreams of moving back to the Midwest, the place of his boyhood, to take a job in his father's company. On the other hand, the bride's family is located in her home state, New Mexico. She may have assumed that the Southwest would be their home. Obviously, for the couple to move abruptly in either direction could be problematic.

This is a question that should be discussed seriously prior to marriage. The bride or groom would be happy in their own familiar area with their family and friends close at hand. The other may feel lonely and lost. The consequence may be dividing in nature unless adequately dealt with prior to marriage and/or such a move.

Bride/Wife's Response:

_____
_____
_____
_____
_____
_____

Groom/Husband's Response:

_____
_____
_____
_____
_____
_____

Negotiations/Decision:

_____
_____
_____
_____
_____

16. **Will we live in an apartment, condo, or single-family dwelling?**

    Often this question seems to answer itself. Couples may marry in an area where single-family dwellings are very high priced. In such cases the couple can only afford an apartment, then later move to a condo while saving money for their dream home. These matters need to be discussed early in the engagement period. If there is a home to be purchased, the questions then becomes where, what type, and under what conditions?

    Bride/Wife's Response:

    _____
    _____
    _____
    _____
    _____
    _____
    _____
    _____

    Groom/Husband's Response:

    _____
    _____
    _____
    _____
    _____
    _____
    _____
    _____

    Negotiations/Decision:

    _____
    _____
    _____
    _____
    _____
    _____
    _____
    _____

17. **Will we rent, lease or purchase? At what point in our marriage, and under what conditions, will we plan to purchase a residence?**

I often watch a television program involving perspective first-time homebuyers. It is interesting to hear the comments of the husband and wife as they look at houses. In most cases, it seems obvious that they have not had a great deal of prior discussion regarding financial limits, number of bedrooms, size of yard, parking, etc. Other crucial matters may include distance from work and access to medical facilities. The latter becomes particularly important when children come into the family.

It is best to discuss these items before marriage. Naturally, the size of a house may be influenced by the size of family the couple plans to have. That topic will be covered in Question 44.

Bride/Wife's Response:

_____
_____
_____
_____
_____
_____
_____

Groom/Husband's Response:

_____
_____
_____
_____
_____

Negotiations/Decision:

_____
_____
_____
_____
_____
_____
_____

18. **How shall we determine the motif for our home—style of furniture, decorating, etc.?**

Most couples that I meet for counseling assume that the woman will make all the decisions related to style, decorating, etc. In my home, it is completely different—I am the decorator. However, I always seek my wife's opinion prior to any major change. The husband and wife may have differing opinions regarding decorating. Both envision what their home should be. Therefore, there should be very early discussion and negotiation.

There have been many comedies built around the situation resulting from a husband who suddenly brings home a moose head to hang over the fireplace or puts a pool table in the dining room. These things need to be discussed—the earlier the better.

Bride/Wife's Response:

_____
_____
_____
_____
_____
_____
_____

Groom/Husband's Response:

_____
_____
_____
_____
_____
_____

Negotiations/Decision:

_____
_____
_____
_____
_____
_____

19. **Under what conditions would we consider living with parents or other relatives?**

    There may be cases where couples move in with relatives and everything works in a cozy fashion. My experience from many counseling sessions gives evidence that usually living with in-laws brings problems.

    I am told that the Chinese have a proverb, "One woman for one house." Study of their society seems to contradict that saying. Nevertheless, I think it is well to keep it in mind. Regardless of the size of the house, one woman in the house seems to work best. This is sometimes well illustrated by the wife's territorial dominance over a particular area, such as the kitchen.

    Obviously, there may be times, during loss of employment or other financial or physical distress, when moving in with parents, or having aging parents move in with you, is unavoidable. In such cases, a clear understanding of participatory and territorial boundaries is an absolute necessity.

    Bride/Wife's Response:

    _____
    _____
    _____
    _____
    _____
    _____

    Groom/Husband's Response:

    _____
    _____
    _____
    _____
    _____

    Negotiations/Decision:

    _____
    _____
    _____
    _____
    _____
    _____

20. **To what extent will we permit our life together to be influenced by parents, siblings, in-laws, or friends?**

The extent of influence by parents on the lives of their married children may range between troublesome and ridiculous. I remember doing premarital counseling with one rather ideal couple. They had everything worked out to their satisfaction. Troublesome areas had been negotiated. All the pieces were in place, including the purchase of a home just a week prior to their wedding. The couple was married in a beautiful ceremony and left for a honeymoon in Hawaii.

The bride's father and mother decided to surprise the couple by remodeling their home while they were on the honeymoon. They returned to find new cabinets, new floors and new fixtures. The father was beaming and the mother was expecting shouts of joy. But the newlyweds were devastated. It was nice but it was not theirs.

Sometimes the influence and intrusion by parents, siblings or friends is more subtle. They just cross the bounds of propriety enough to cause irritation between the husband and wife by the little things they do and say—a girlfriend speaks to the wife concerning something she heard about the husband; or a gentleman friend advises the husband on child rearing when the couple has already made agreement on such matters.

Bride/Wife's Response:

_____

_____

_____

_____

_____

Groom/Husband's Response:

_____

_____

_____

_____

_____

Negotiations/Decision:

_____

_____

_____

_____

_____

21. **What will we consider to be a reasonable amount of time for each of us to devote to poker with the boys, shopping with the girls, clubs, sports, etc.?**

There is a generally accepted old saying, "Absence makes the heart grow fonder." That proverbial advice does not always work in a marriage. The amount of time that each party spends away for entertainment purposes, not including the spouse, can, and often does, become a source of irritation. Just what is the right amount of time to spend with friends and not include the spouse? The answer depends upon the couple and conversation, conversation, conversation. The number one guiding rule is: if it is aggravating or just a little irritating, talk about it.

Bride/Wife's Response:

_____
_____
_____
_____
_____
_____
_____
_____

Groom/Husband's Response:

_____
_____
_____
_____
_____
_____
_____
_____

Negotiations/Decision:

_____
_____
_____
_____
_____
_____
_____
_____

22. **How will we determine the division of labor around the house; cooking, cleaning, yard work, etc.?**

There is no answer that works in every situation. If the husband works an eight-hour, five or six day week, then it seems obvious that the wife, if she is not working outside the home, should do the bulk of cleaning, cooking and laundry. It continues logically, that the husband should be of help when he is at home, particularly after children come into the marriage. Being a mother is also a full time job, seven days a week, 24 hours a day. What if both work? The answer comes through discussion and negotiation. Even discussion will not work in these matters unless feelings are put forth honestly and openly.

I enjoy doing work around the house. I particularly like to run the vacuum, clean the garage, and tidy up the closets. Now that my wife and I are both retired, I do those things. I do not like to dust, so Donna does all the dusting, the cooking, the shopping, cleans the bathroom, etc. In our case, we each do what we sort of enjoy. The answer came easily for us.

In marriage, the term *women's work* or *masculine duties* should be forgotten and the division of labor should result from a realistic look at what needs to be done. Then the work should be lovingly divided.

Bride/Wife's Response:

_____

_____

_____

_____

_____

Groom/Husband's Response:

_____

_____

_____

_____

_____

Negotiations/Decision:

_____

_____

_____

_____

_____

23. **What boundaries will we establish to protect our sacred space?**

I have found that many divorces come about as the result of the husband and wife permitting invasion of their sacred space or because one or both of them violate the boundaries.

Marital sacred space is that area of life, both physical and emotional, that belongs just to the husband and wife. Neither husband nor wife should venture outside the sacred space without the full knowledge and consent of the other. It follows, then, that the bride and groom, long before marriage, should completely define the limits of their sacred space.

Sometimes problems arise and either husband or wife becomes terribly frustrated. For comfort they run to mother or a friend. This is a violation of the sacred space agreement. The matter should be discussed privately between the two. Only in cases where counseling is needed should the couple go outside their sacred space, unless they decide to do so together.

Obviously, the question that arises following an attempt of invasion into a sacred space is, which one should take care of the matter. The answer is really simple but should be agreed upon by the couple. If the intruder into your marital sacred space is a family member, a friend or associate of the husband, he should engage in the necessary confrontation to solve the problem. If the intruder is related to the wife, the problem is hers to solve with the husband quietly supporting.

Bride/Wife's Response:

_____
_____
_____
_____

Groom/Husband's Response:

_____
_____
_____
_____

Negotiations/Decision:

_____
_____
_____
_____

CHAPTER V

Financial Matters

A couple entering marriage has no guarantee of financial stability. Crises come. Now, early in the Twenty-First Century, our country is facing financial difficulties. There is a high rate of unemployment. Some couples that have been married just a few years had good jobs at the time of the wedding. Now, one or both may be unemployed. Such conditions may cause a strain on the relationship.

There is no way to assure that money-related problems will not arise, but planning and agreement on financial matters, prior to marriage, make the good times better and the bad times more bearable. The possibility of marital upset, due to financial problems, may be lessened by giving proper consideration to the following topics.

24. **What are my expectations regarding a standard of living?**

Both the bride and groom must answer this question for themselves. Then they should share their expectations with one another. Sometimes individual expectations may differ so broadly that they limit the probability of a happy and lasting relationship.

It has often been said that love makes for strange bedfellows. The suggestion is that sufficient love can overcome substantial differences. However, vastly differing views can end a relationship. If the bride has hopes of traveling the world with first class accommodations, eating her meals in five-star restaurants and shopping on Rodeo Drive, she may be hard pressed to find joy with a gentleman who has much simpler desires. It is of great importance that couples discuss their expectations. It is generally agreed that things do not cause happiness. However, in the midst of high expectations, the lack of things can sometimes cause serious problems.

Bride/Wife's Response:

_____
_____
_____
_____
_____
_____
_____

Groom/Husband's Response:

_____
_____
_____
_____
_____
_____
_____

Negotiations/Decision:

_____
_____
_____
_____
_____
_____
_____

25. **Will we have one joint bank account or individual accounts?**

As simple as this decision seems, it is, in many instances, the cause of major disruption in a marriage. There is no logical reason requiring one bank account as opposed to each having their individual accounts. On the other hand, separate finances may give rise to doubt and suspicion, thus causing a strain on the relationship.

I have counseled with couples where each have had their own individual banking account for many years prior to marriage and they chose to continue with individual accounts. I noticed in their conversations with each other and with me, as their counselor, the phrases, *my money* and *your money*. Individual accounts seem to cause a division of financial purpose. Obviously, with separate accounts, the question continually arises, who pays for what?

So, there is no absolute answer as to right or wrong of personal or joint accounts. It is a matter of individual choice. However, please be aware that the route of individual accounts can be problematic. Communication, communication, communication.

Bride/Wife's Response:

_____

_____

_____

_____

_____

_____

Groom/Husband's Response:

_____

_____

_____

_____

_____

Negotiations/Decision:

_____

_____

_____

_____

_____

26. **How many credit cards shall we have and what will be their financial limit?**

In the excitement of being newly married and the necessity to purchase furniture, household goods, etc., many couples over extend themselves by accepting and using too many credit cards. It is easy to spend and charge to a credit card, but within thirty days or so, the bill comes. The more cards, the greater the tendency to spend, and the larger amount of monthly indebtedness. Add the over-all debt and the high interest rate on credit cards and obviously there are problems.

It is best for the engaged couple, long before the wedding, to make firm decisions on standard of living, banking, and the number of credit cards they should hold. Even with one or two cards, it is easy to over spend. Decide in advance what your maximum limits on credit should be.

Bride/Wife's Response:

_____
_____
_____
_____
_____
_____

Groom/Husband's Response:

_____
_____
_____
_____
_____
_____

Negotiations/Decision:

_____
_____
_____
_____
_____

27. **Which person will be responsible for paying the bills and record keeping?**

    This was an easy decision in my family. Prior to marriage, my wife was my Administrative Assistant and Secretary. She paid my bills and kept all records. I liked it that way. After marriage, we continued the process because for us it works. She likes to deal with the numbers. I don't.

    For some couples, this matter will be a problem. Both may wish to be in control of the finances. That kind of plan will work but they must control together. It requires time to discuss expenses, bank statements, financial records, budget, and tax preparation.

    My experience, both personally and from years of marriage counseling, seems to indicate that it is best if one party takes care of bill payment and record keeping, assuming he or she keeps the mate sufficiently informed.

    Bride/Wife's Response:

    _____
    _____
    _____
    _____
    _____
    _____
    _____

    Groom/Husband's Response:

    _____
    _____
    _____
    _____
    _____
    _____
    _____

    Negotiations/Decision:

    _____
    _____
    _____
    _____
    _____
    _____
    _____

28. **We will agree on an annual budget early in our marriage, if possible, prior to the wedding ceremony.**

    A budget is extremely important, although quite aggravating. There always seems to be something needed which does not fall within the budget. The taxes and rent columns are troublingly high and the food and entertainment allotment always seems to be insufficient.

    In the marriage, although the minister has recently pronounced that you, as a couple have become one, there will be differences in what you feel to be priority. So, rather than discuss every expenditure item, do it the easy way. Establish a budget and live within it to the best of your ability. Obviously, exceptions to move outside the budget can always be made jointly, if there is an emergency or other sufficiently necessary cause.

    If the bride and groom each have their own credit cards and bank accounts, living within a budget is more difficult.

    Bride/Wife's Response:

    _____
    _____
    _____
    _____
    _____
    _____
    _____

    Groom/Husband's Response:

    _____
    _____
    _____
    _____
    _____
    _____
    _____

    Negotiations/Decision:

    _____
    _____
    _____
    _____
    _____
    _____
    _____

29. **How much may each of us spend without accountability to the other?**

The actual dollar amount is dependent upon income and budget. Nevertheless, it is wise for every couple, regardless of funds available, to establish an amount that neither of them will exceed without talking with the spouse.

The whole question revolves around priorities within the marriage; and, of course, priorities may only be established and maintained with full and open participation of each party. This matter is more easily controlled if there is only one bank account for the household.

Bride/Wife's Response:

_____
_____
_____
_____
_____
_____
_____
_____

Groom/Husband's Response:

_____
_____
_____
_____
_____
_____
_____
_____

Negotiations/Decision:

_____
_____
_____
_____
_____
_____
_____
_____

30. **What percentage of our income will be placed into savings?**

Although there are exceptions, most newly married couples are too much into fun and excitement to have a true interest in a savings account—they are young, and there will be time.

There will be emergencies when funds are desperately needed. If there are no savings, then borrowing becomes necessary. Borrowing requires an additional line item in the budget for payback with interest. That hurts. Saving is a good thing. Talk about it, agree on it and do it from the very beginning.

It seems that the best rule is to save by percentage. For instance, ten percent of income is to be placed in a savings account each month. Make it the first ten per cent. Otherwise it may not happen. The couple that saves only what is left at the end of the month, seldom saves at all.

Bride/Wife's Response:

_____
_____
_____
_____
_____
_____
_____

Groom/Husband's Response:

_____
_____
_____
_____
_____
_____
_____

Negotiations/Decision:

_____
_____
_____
_____
_____
_____
_____

31. **How much will we allocate for charitable contributions, including church, hospitals, your alma mater, and other helpful organizations?**

    The answer to a question of giving is altogether personal. Some couples choose to give little; others give a lot. Whatever the case, there must be agreement and it must be in the budget.

    Furthering this question, will you give small amounts to many organizations or support one organization working in the area of your special interest. As the result of years of giving, Donna and I have found that supporting a few causes quite well is more satisfying than sprinkling a small amount across many organizations.

    As a general rule, I think giving is good. Hopefully, the needy benefit from the result of giving. My wife and I have found that giving is gratifying.

    Bride/Wife's Response:

    _____
    _____
    _____
    _____
    _____
    _____
    _____

    Groom/Husband's Response:

    _____
    _____
    _____
    _____
    _____
    _____
    _____

    Negotiations/Decision:

    _____
    _____
    _____
    _____
    _____
    _____
    _____

32. **What items will we consider to be essential, and/or non-essential?**

When a budget is prepared, there are certain columns and line items which are absolutely necessary—utilities, rent or mortgage, taxes and insurance. Other items may vary. The food column may flux substantially according to the number of times you eat out. So, it is necessary that the bride and groom agree generally on what will be considered essential. This matter often requires negotiation. Some women may consider manicures to be essential. Men usually clip their own fingernails. So, whether or not a service or purchase is necessary may not be a matter of easy agreement. Discuss it.

Sometimes, as long as it doesn't happen too often as to upset your budget completely, engaging as a couple in a non-essential item such as a weekend away or a cruise can add sparkle to a marriage.

Bride/Wife's Response:

_____
_____
_____
_____
_____
_____
_____

Groom/Husband's Response:

_____
_____
_____
_____
_____
_____
_____

Negotiations/Decision:

_____
_____
_____
_____
_____
_____

33. **How much will we budget for entertainment, recreation, hobbies, etc.**

    This is one of the highly touchy subjects in budgeting, particularly if one spouse feels the need to live frugally in order to save more money, and the other gets great joy from recreation and hobbies. There is no right answer. This matter requires a lot of discussion, understanding and negotiation. This is an additional justification for fully understanding the bride/groom's areas of interest prior to the wedding.

    Bride/Wife's Response:

    _____
    _____
    _____
    _____
    _____
    _____
    _____
    _____

    Groom/Husband's Response:

    _____
    _____
    _____
    _____
    _____
    _____
    _____
    _____

    Negotiations/Decision:

    _____
    _____
    _____
    _____
    _____
    _____
    _____
    _____

34. **How will decisions be made regarding major purchases such as appliances, furniture, and automobiles?**

    Couples must agree on what is most needed, when to purchase it and how payment will be made. All these matters must work in concert. For instance, both husband and wife may agree on the need and the particular item. But one may be willing to go in debt and the other insists on waiting until there is cash for payment. These matters may not be definitively discussed before marriage; however, it is necessary that the bride and groom recognize the possible pitfalls involved, even when buying a much-needed item.

    Bride/Wife's Response:

    _____
    _____
    _____
    _____
    _____
    _____
    _____
    _____

    Groom/Husband's Response:

    _____
    _____
    _____
    _____
    _____
    _____
    _____

    Negotiations/Decision:

    _____
    _____
    _____
    _____
    _____
    _____
    _____

35. **Will we have one automobile or two? Will we lease or purchase?**

Often, prior to marriage, both the bride and groom are employed and own their own automobile. It is easy, then, to take the two vehicles into the marriage. However, each vehicle requires insurance, fuel, and maintenance. So the decision regarding the number of automobiles is both one of convenience and finance.

When I was planning to purchase my first car, my father said to me, "Son, remember the purpose of an automobile is simply to get you from point A to point B." That was many years ago. No longer is an automobile considered simply transportation. It is also a status symbol.

When my wife and I lived in California, we each had our own car. Both cars were jointly owned, but one was considered mine and the other was Donna's. That's the way most couples operate in California. When we moved to the Midwest, it was obvious we did not really need two cars. After all, we go places together now. Admittedly, there are times when we have to take care in booking doctor appointments, haircuts, etc., in order to continue this practice comfortably. It works. One car costs much less than two.

Bride/Wife's Response:

_____
_____
_____
_____
_____
_____

Groom/Husband's Response:

_____
_____
_____
_____
_____
_____

Negotiations/Decision:

_____
_____
_____
_____
_____

36. **How will we regard the use of personal funds, assuming one party inherits money or brings substantial funds into the marriage?**

During my years of marriage counseling, I found that this item seemed to be the cause of many problems. One party brings substantial personal funds into the marriage or parents die and leave an inheritance to either the husband or wife. In some states there are legal issues related to inheritance. For our purposes, we will consider only emotional and relational issues.

Prior to marriage, it is important to acknowledge that the money of one essentially becomes the money of both. It is tradition and generally expected. That's the reason the clergy person asked both to say, "With all my worldly goods I do thee endow." That vow is intended to eliminate nitpicking later over who owns what.

If, for some reason, one party wishes to maintain ownership of a block of money, that intent should be clearly stated and completely accepted by the couple prior to coming together for married life. Money is important. Handle it carefully. Often your future depends upon it. Nevertheless, wealth is secondary to a loving relationship.

Bride/Wife's Response:

_____

_____

_____

_____

_____

_____

Groom/Husband's Response:

_____

_____

_____

_____

_____

_____

Negotiations/Decision:

_____

_____

_____

_____

_____

_____

37. **Are we in full agreement regarding financial liability that either person may bring into the marriage—personal debt, mortgages, student loans, etc.?**

    This matter, too, is the cause of many sticky issues. It is far more common than personal wealth discussed in the previous question.

    All debts of any kind, regardless of how they came about, should be fully acknowledged and openly discussed prior to marriage. I have known cases where one party had so much debt the other decided not to continue plans for marriage. It is easy in our economy to leave college with personal debt and student loans in the amount of tens of thousands of dollars. Some brides/grooms may consider such indebtedness more than they wish to accept.

    Bride/Wife's Response:

    _____
    _____
    _____
    _____
    _____
    _____
    _____
    _____

    Groom/Husband's Response:

    _____
    _____
    _____
    _____
    _____
    _____
    _____
    _____

    Negotiations/Decision:

    _____
    _____
    _____
    _____
    _____
    _____
    _____
    _____

38. **Who will be our legal counsel?**

Every newly married couple needs to decide on an attorney. Legal counsel is helpful when signing long-term contracts, purchasing property, beginning a business, entering into a partnership, making a will, or in more serious legal matters such as a lawsuit. Don't wait for a particular need. Agree on legal counsel early, even before the ceremony, if possible.

As with many of the questions in this document, matters such as deciding on legal counsel may seem to be one that is easy to delay. After all, there are no pressing legal problems now. However, it could happen as quickly as a lawsuit as the result of someone falling or being cut with a broken champagne glass at the wedding reception.

Bride/Wife's Response:

_____
_____
_____
_____
_____
_____
_____
_____

Groom/Husband's Response:

_____
_____
_____
_____
_____
_____
_____

Negotiations/Decision:

_____
_____
_____
_____
_____
_____
_____

39. **At what point will we plan for the distribution of assets in case of disability or death—wills, trusts, etc.?**

The answer is simple. Create wills, trusts, and other necessary legal matters, according to the laws of your state of residence, as early as possible following the wedding. Most people think about wills as having to do with distribution of stuff at the end of their life. Such reasoning is not all bad. The catch is, the end of life comes, sadly to say, sometimes long before we are old. In recent years, brides or grooms have been lost at sea during a honeymoon cruise. Unfortunately, untimely events happen. Prepare.

Bride/Wife's Response:

_____

_____

_____

_____

_____

_____

Groom/Husband's Response:

_____

_____

_____

_____

_____

_____

Negotiations/Decision:

_____

_____

_____

_____

_____

_____

40. **How will we reach agreement regarding investments—stocks, bonds, purchase of property, etc.?**

First, and foremost, making purchases and stock investments should only be made with the full agreement of both parties. Of equal importance, follow this simple rule. Do not make stock investments above a financial amount that you are willing and able to lose in the worse case scenario. Such investments are a bet on the future. The future is never fully known.

Bride/Wife's Response:

_____
_____
_____
_____
_____
_____
_____
_____

Groom/Husband's Response:

_____
_____
_____
_____
_____
_____
_____

Negotiations/Decision:

_____
_____
_____
_____
_____
_____
_____
_____

41. **Will we have a financial advisor? If so, who?**

    If you decide, as a couple, to make stock or bonds investments, professional counsel is advisable. Be wise in selecting an advisor. Do not, in any case, select a friend or family member as your financial advisor. From the pool of hundreds of other advisors available, check out their track record—how have they been doing for others? Remember, beyond all else, brokers are sales people. They make their living by selling.

    Bride/Wife's Response:

    _____
    _____
    _____
    _____
    _____
    _____
    _____
    _____

    Groom/Husband's Response:

    _____
    _____
    _____
    _____
    _____
    _____
    _____

    Negotiations/Decision:

    _____
    _____
    _____
    _____
    _____
    _____
    _____

42. **How will we establish limits on rent, household accessories, etc.?**

    I purposely put this question last. Obviously it involves many of your answers to earlier questions. As you discuss this question, separate logic from emotion. Agree to do so continually. As an example, suppose you are looking for an apartment. You find one that is ideal, but it is several hundred dollars a month beyond your established limit. This calls for an important decision. Will you live within your budget or forget it with this first big decision. The same problem will present itself with the purchase of household items. Appliances come in different price ranges. Perhaps the all stainless steel refrigerator will not be within your budget the first time around. Communicate, communicate, communicate. These are matters that make or break.

    Bride/Wife's Response:

    _____
    _____
    _____
    _____
    _____
    _____
    _____
    _____

    Groom/Husband's Response:

    _____
    _____
    _____
    _____
    _____
    _____
    _____
    _____

    Negotiations/Decision:

    _____
    _____
    _____
    _____
    _____
    _____
    _____

CHAPTER VI

When Children Come

Few young couples are completely prepared for the arrival of a third party into their relationship. Although children are a natural result, and considered by many to be the fulfillment of the relationship, their presence sometimes puts a strain on the marriage. Schedules are changed, priorities must be rearranged, the couple that once devoted their entire lives to each other, now has a new object of affection. Although wonderful and a miracle of God, the addition of a child into the marriage relationship requires planning, understanding, patience and love.

Before the marriage ceremony, before the preparation of a nursery or the purchase of diapers, the bride and groom should seriously consider the following questions.

43. **Do we wish to have children?**

A young couple walked into my office for a scheduled appointment. He was in the final year of law school. She worked in the movie industry. They were an attractive couple. Their dress and demeanor smacked of prosperity. Then came the shocker. The husband said, "Dr. Sago, we are here to work out a divorce." He went on to explain that before they were married, the bride had made it clear that she did not wish to have children. The groom agreed. No children.

The couple had been married three years. For her, one part of their future was clear—no children. The husband had changed his mind. For some reason, which he did not fully understand, now he desperately wanted a family. All negotiation had failed. There seemed to be only one answer—divorce.

Our session that evening lasted about two hours. They left more than good friends; they were still in love. But there was one blaring disagreement—children! The couple agreed on divorce.

I tell about this couple to hopefully make one point clear. Prior to marriage, state openly and honestly how you feel about having children.

Bride/Wife's Response:

_____

_____

_____

_____

_____

_____

Groom/Husband's Response:

_____

_____

_____

_____

_____

_____

Negotiations/Decision:

_____

_____

_____

_____

_____

44. **Agree on the number of children you feel to be appropriate for your family.**

The birth of a child is not always a planned event. Pregnancies often just happen. Nevertheless, it is best prior to marriage to agree upon the size of your family. Circumstances may change and the number increase. But planning is good, for one very simple reason. Suppose the groom comes from a very large family. His childhood was a happy one and he hopes to have a large family. On the other hand, the bride feels that one or two children is sufficient for a complete family.

Don't go into the marriage with such a difference of opinion. Decide on the approximate number of children you both feel to be most desirable. Given modern birth control, it can probably work out that way.

Bride/Wife's Response:

_____

_____

_____

_____

_____

_____

_____

Groom/Husband's Response:

_____

_____

_____

_____

_____

_____

Negotiations/Decision:

_____

_____

_____

_____

_____

_____

_____

45. **If we are unable to have children, will we consider other options?**

For most couples, childbirth comes as planned, sometimes unplanned. Others find, for physical reasons, the husband is unable to father a child or the wife cannot conceive. Such conditions bring great disappointment. Adoption, in vitro fertilization or a surrogate mother may be the couple's only hope for a child. It is best to discuss your feelings regarding these alternatives prior to marriage. Such a decision is not easy in a time of emotional stress.

On this item, I have one suggestion for the couple that may consider alternatives to natural childbirth. Talk to other couples that have taken that route. Ask about the joys, the problems, and perhaps heartbreaks that have been experienced in the process. In some cases, the cost may be a limiting factor.

Bride/Wife's Response:

_____
_____
_____
_____
_____
_____
_____
_____

Groom/Husband's Response:

_____
_____
_____
_____
_____
_____

Negotiations/Decision:

_____
_____
_____
_____
_____
_____
_____

46. **Prior to the arrival of children, we will study methods of discipline and agree on ways for guidance and correction.**

Prior to marriage, it is difficult to plan precise methods for disciplining children. Nevertheless, your feelings regarding methods for guidance and correction should be discussed. When one parent is strict and the other permissive, the result is conflict. Unfortunately, the children, themselves, are often witnesses to the disagreement.

Discipline becomes difficult and sometimes nearly impossible as the result of both parents working, and/or placing the child with a relative or in a child-care facility. In such cases, the child may be more influenced by others than by the parents. Consequently, the parents must be in agreement concerning methods and extent of discipline, not only between themselves, but by relatives or caregivers.

Bride/Wife's Response:

_____
_____
_____
_____
_____
_____
_____
_____

Groom/Husband's Response:

_____
_____
_____
_____
_____
_____
_____

Negotiations/Decision:

_____
_____
_____
_____
_____
_____
_____
_____

47. **We will serve as positive examples to our children, including our choices regarding alcohol, tobacco, drugs, etc.**

It is not uncommon for the bride or groom or both to use alcohol and/or illegal drugs. There may be serious consequences when the habits are carried into marriage. Certain drugs can have a devastating affect on pregnancy and the physical and mental wellbeing of children. Even in cases when there is normal birth and children are mentally and physically in an acceptable progression, the mother and father's habits, if continued, may have a devastating affect on family life.

The engagement period affords a wonderful opportunity for discussion, a pledge of dedication and love, and a promise of becoming and/or staying clean for the benefit of each other and future children.

Bride/Wife's Response:

_____
_____
_____
_____
_____
_____
_____

Groom/Husband's Response:

_____
_____
_____
_____
_____
_____

Negotiations/Decision:

_____
_____
_____
_____
_____
_____
_____

48. **Agree that certain issues should not be discussed in the presence of children, family or friends.**

    Frustrated parents sometimes conclude that their children do not listen. Just the opposite is true. Children may not listen precisely in the way and at the time you would like. But they do listen very well, particularly to conversations between husband and wife pertaining to items such as financial problems, criticism of friends, a mother-in-law, politics, etc. Small children can become very frustrated by hearing parents frantically discuss their financial woes. Don't do it. Such things should stay just between the two of you.

    Bride/Wife's Response:

    _____
    _____
    _____
    _____
    _____
    _____
    _____
    _____

    Groom/Husband's Response:

    _____
    _____
    _____
    _____
    _____
    _____
    _____
    _____

    Negotiations/Decision:

    _____
    _____
    _____
    _____
    _____
    _____
    _____
    _____

49. **Since too much may be hurtful, we will agree on how much is enough for our children—toys, sports, activities, TV, etc.**

Most children have far too much—too many clothes, toys, too much sports equipment, too many activities, and too much TV. Too much stuff becomes frustrating.

Often children accumulate dozens of toys. Many of the toys are given by parents in an attempt to compensate for the lack of quality time between parent and child. Giving the child a new baseball can never be equal to attending their baseball game.

Bride/Wife's Response:

_____
_____
_____
_____
_____
_____
_____
_____

Groom/Husband's Response:

_____
_____
_____
_____
_____
_____
_____

Negotiations/Decision:

_____
_____
_____
_____
_____
_____
_____

50. **We will agree to make the education of our children a priority in family life.**

Parents, by example, establish levels of expectation for the children—reading is good, history is exciting, museums are fun and every adventure is an educational opportunity. Children are naturally inquisitive. They love to learn. Sometimes they ask hard questions. Remember, if they are able to ask the question, they are probably ready to receive the answer.

Bride/Wife's Response:

_____
_____
_____
_____
_____
_____
_____

Groom/Husband's Response:

_____
_____
_____
_____
_____

Negotiations/Decision:

_____
_____
_____
_____
_____
_____

51. **Who will we name as guardian for our children in the case of our disability or demise?**

Very few couples choose to act on this subject. Naturally, there is a feeling that they are young, they are healthy, and the threat of disability or death is distant. That is not always the case. Accidents, sickness and natural disasters occur. Sometimes children are left without parents. Where do they go? What is the plan for their welfare? Usually, the answer is none.

Seriously consider this matter. Who? What person specifically would you wish to raise your children in case of your inability to do so? That is the first step. Think of the right person. Then, it is necessary to talk with that person and their spouse to gain their permission to take on such an obligation should the need arise. Next, talk with your attorney and make legal arrangements to assure that your child will be with the guardian of your choice.

Bride/Wife's Response:

_____
_____
_____
_____
_____
_____
_____

Groom/Husband's Response:

_____
_____
_____
_____
_____
_____
_____

Negotiations/Decision:

_____
_____
_____
_____
_____
_____

Chapter VII

Religion

Religious faith may serve as a bonding agent for the husband and wife and provide a safeguard for their sacred space. On occasion, religion may be a cause that divides. The bride and groom that fail to discuss religious matters and come to full agreement, may eventually find themselves at odds with each other and their families.

Families of an engaged couple sometimes play a crucial and devastating role when it comes to religion. There can be problems when a son or daughter marries outside the religious faith of the family. Some family units that hold a very conservative religious view tend to be more insistent that their offspring, even when married, continue in their family ideology. Such families may, at times, attempt to influence the religious upbringing of the grandchildren.

Before the wedding ceremony, discuss issues relating to religion. Family religious values will play a part in your discussion. However, it is absolutely necessary that the two of you decide how you will practice your faith and train your children.

52. **Do we agree on the practice of religious beliefs?**

Assuming the bride and groom have been raised in the same church and wish to continue in that religious setting, there should be no conflict, or so it seems. The actual problem may be that they will have no religion at all to call their own. It may simply be an inherited or borrowed religion and their children will be born into it and continue the practice.

If the religion selected is that of one set of parents, and in conflict with the other, there may be additional problems. Consequently, many couples from differing religious backgrounds choose, during the engagement period, to visit different churches and then select a church home for themselves that is different from either of their families.

Bride/Wife's Response:

_____
_____
_____
_____
_____
_____
_____
_____

Groom/Husband's Response:

_____
_____
_____
_____
_____
_____
_____

Negotiations/Decision:

_____
_____
_____
_____
_____
_____
_____

53. **Will we openly discuss our religious preferences?**

The answer to this question must be yes. The bride and groom, both before and after the wedding ceremony, are a team. A team should not be divided.

Not only must a married couple be open and honest in their discussion of religious feelings, they must both protect this part of their marriage as sacred space and guard against the intrusion of well-meaning relatives and friends.

Bride/Wife's Response:

_____
_____
_____
_____
_____
_____
_____
_____

Groom/Husband's Response:

_____
_____
_____
_____
_____
_____
_____

Negotiations/Decision:

_____
_____
_____
_____
_____
_____
_____

54. **If we cannot agree on religious matters, can we agree on a neutral position?**

    In most cases, the answer is absolutely. We will be neutral. The problem is that neutrality tends toward nothingness. In a neutral position, you will be even more open to well-meaning fanatical family members and friends who will challenge you to accept their belief system. Further, and perhaps of even greater importance, if you choose religious neutrality, what will happen when children come into the family? Grandpas and grandmas become very enthusiastically active at that time.

    Bride/Wife's Response:

    _____
    _____
    _____
    _____
    _____
    _____
    _____

    Groom/Husband's Response:

    _____
    _____
    _____
    _____
    _____
    _____
    _____

    Negotiations/Decision:

    _____
    _____
    _____
    _____
    _____
    _____
    _____

55. **When children come, how will you manage their religious training?**

Neutrality will not work. To confine their religious exposure to one church seems limiting and unfair. How will your family handle religious holidays? Your children want to know. You, the bride and groom, soon to be mother and dad, must decide.

Bride/Wife's Response:

_____
_____
_____
_____
_____
_____
_____

Groom/Husband's Response:

_____
_____
_____
_____
_____
_____
_____

Negotiations/Decision:

_____
_____
_____
_____
_____
_____
_____

56. **At what age will you tell your children about God?**

Of all the matters regarding religion and children, this is the most important. Will you be honest and open in teaching your child or will you follow the dictates of a particular church organization? That is the primary and very difficult question.

Discuss this item early, long before children. Decide on a method to help your children acknowledge God without fear and with thanksgiving for our beautiful world.

Bride/Wife's Response:

_____
_____
_____
_____
_____
_____
_____
_____

Groom/Husband's Response:

_____
_____
_____
_____
_____
_____
_____

Negotiations/Decision:

_____
_____
_____
_____
_____
_____
_____

57. **Will you permit and guide your children in differing, perhaps conflicting religious experiences?**

Children who are raised in a religious family usually adopt that religion without question. In other words, the child will simply take religion for granted and not feel the need for serious thought.

Beginning about age 10, I had the advantage of attending all three of the small churches in my hometown—the Methodist on Sunday morning, the Church of the Nazarene on Sunday night and a Pentecostal Holiness Church on special occasions. Each of those churches contributed significantly to my spiritual understanding. As a young adult, I chose a church home; interestingly, it was none of those three.

Bride/Wife's Response:

_____
_____
_____
_____
_____
_____
_____
_____

Groom/Husband's Response:

_____
_____
_____
_____
_____
_____
_____

Negotiations/Decision:

_____
_____
_____
_____
_____
_____
_____

58. **Will we, as a family, attend worship regularly and make religion a priority in our lives?**

   During the last few decades, many teenagers and young adults have ignored the church. There are, of course, many reasons. Chief among them—the hectic pace of life, so many things to do and entertainment on every hand. Not so many years ago, the church, particularly in a smaller community, was the center of activity.

   Children should learn from their parents that the love of God is personal and that giving thanks daily is good. Beyond that, your child, as he/she matures, should be encouraged to make choices for themselves.

   Bride/Wife's Response:

   _____
   _____
   _____
   _____
   _____
   _____
   _____
   _____

   Groom/Husband's Response:

   _____
   _____
   _____
   _____
   _____
   _____
   _____

   Negotiations/Decision:

   _____
   _____
   _____
   _____
   _____
   _____
   _____

CHAPTER VIII

The Second Marriage

Couples, where one or both have been previously married, face a particular set of challenges: financial and emotional baggage that may be carried from the previous life into the new relationship. Financial baggage is easily identified and may be comfortably resolved if communication is open and honest. Emotional baggage is far more complicated. Much like actual travel luggage, emotional baggage must be unpacked—part of it thrown in the trash and other items must be sorted out and put away. Serious problems occur when either husband or wife retrieves items from the emotional baggage and brings them directly into the new life situation; i.e., comparing the new spouse with the former one or passing judgment on a present situation by contrasting it with incidents from a previous marriage. Problems are often multiplied when there is a blending of families. In such cases, the couple should give serious consideration to the following topics.

59. **We will attempt, with the help of counseling when necessary, to reduce emotional and financial baggage carried over from previous relationships.**

   Baggage, whether emotional or material, (defined as concerns, cares, fears, failures, debt, etc.) is carried into a new relationship by a previously married person. We cannot completely forget the past. On the other hand, we should not permit the past to govern our present and future. Agree early in your relationship to be understanding, knowing that there is a past and obviously some baggage. Emotional baggage is much like other baggage—until you unpack the bag and put all the contents in their proper places, the matter will be troublesome. So, together, unpack your emotional baggage, share it with deep feelings, crying and tears, whatever it takes, to become clean emotionally.

   Bride/Wife's Response:

   _____
   _____
   _____
   _____
   _____
   _____
   _____
   _____

   Groom/Husband's Response:

   _____
   _____
   _____
   _____
   _____
   _____
   _____
   _____

   Negotiations/Decision:

   _____
   _____
   _____
   _____
   _____
   _____
   _____
   _____

60. **We will make no assumptions with regard to our spouse based on our previous marital experience.**

This topic relates to the previous matter—baggage. It is easy to pass judgment on a new spouse by drawing on unhappy experiences from your past as evidence for the present or future happenings. Agree together that the past is prologue. Now all things are new. Build that new life together with honesty and open communication.

Bride/Wife's Response:

_____

_____

_____

_____

_____

_____

_____

_____

Groom/Husband's Response:

_____

_____

_____

_____

_____

_____

_____

_____

Negotiations/Decision:

_____

_____

_____

_____

_____

_____

_____

_____

61. **We will agree on the discipline of minor children by the new parent.**

In a second marriage, the greatest adjustment is on the part of children. They are in a new place with a new person as a parent. That new person receives the love and attention of their birth parent, which was formerly all theirs. Consequently, there is often resentment. The problem multiplies when the new parent disciplines the adopted child. The child then turns to the birth parent. Parents, both new and old, clash. This can be devastating. Work things out prior to the marriage.

Bride/Wife's Response:

_____
_____
_____
_____
_____
_____
_____

Groom/Husband's Response:

_____
_____
_____
_____
_____
_____

Negotiations/Decision:

_____
_____
_____
_____
_____
_____

62. **We will agree upon methods to facilitate fairness and equality among the children of both partners.**

     Sometimes new partners each have children of about the same age. Fairness and equality become paramount. It is easy when considering the previous question, to simply conclude that each parent will discipline their own child/children. It will not work. One parent may be a strict disciplinarian and the other permissive. Immediately, the new stepchildren sense inequality in the family. Discipline, time, attention and chores must be spread equally among the children.

     Bride/Wife's Response:

     _____
     _____
     _____
     _____
     _____
     _____
     _____
     _____

     Groom/Husband's Response:

     _____
     _____
     _____
     _____
     _____
     _____
     _____

     Negotiations/Decision:

     _____
     _____
     _____
     _____
     _____
     _____
     _____

63. **We will establish *family meetings* as a means to facilitate union in the new relationship.**

   In a second marriage, the parents may wish to establish *family meetings*—a time when all members of the family gather around the table to discuss important matters. Those subjects may include fairness and equality among the children, an explanation on the part of parents when special attention must be given to one child, and to provide each family member an opportunity to express their feelings. These meetings may be on a particular night following dinner. After the dishes are cleared, all members come back to the table for family meeting. Obviously, rules of decorum must be established and strictly enforced.

   Bride/Wife's Response:

   _____
   _____
   _____
   _____
   _____
   _____
   _____
   _____

   Groom/Husband's Response:

   _____
   _____
   _____
   _____
   _____
   _____
   _____

   Negotiations/Decision:

   _____
   _____
   _____
   _____
   _____
   _____
   _____
   _____

CHAPTER IX

Nurturing the Marriage

Your marriage can be glorious! You can wake up every morning happy, looking forward to the day together with a type of youthful excitement regardless of your age. But it is totally up to you.

Strong and happy marriages do not just happen! Marriage requires planning and cooperative effort on the part of both husband and wife. Successful marriages must be given constant attention and daily loving care.

In marriage counseling, I worked with a couple who illustrated the points above very well. Both husband and wife were attractive people and seemed dedicated to each other, but the wife described the marriage as being "dull." After an hour or so, and a lot of shallow conversation on their part, we got to the crux of the matter. The husband was an automobile enthusiast. When it came to his car, he was compulsive, always polishing and cleaning and improving it. He never missed a checkup or scheduled repair and all too often had a total detailing for his prize possession. Finally, reality hit us like a bolt of lightening. That was it! His car had become his prized possession. His wife felt that she had been moved to second place, that a machine had replaced her in his affection. I know this sounds corny, almost too dumb to be true. But it happened. And, it happens over and over, if not with cars with other objects, habits and sports interest.

Wives are not immune from this problem of substitution. I have worked with women who become enthralled, perhaps possessed, with their love for shopping—shoes in particular. In other cases, women become possessed by social interests, their clubs, sororities, *or their church*. Their marriage and sometimes the children fall to second place.

You, both of you, must nurture your marriage. Marriage requires daily attention. There will probably be times when your marriage is not romantic. There will be tough times, communication problems and disagreements that require patience and understanding. Nevertheless, to claim the ultimate prize—a glorious marriage—both husband and wife must be faithful, loving, and give daily attention to nurturing the relationship.

64. **Agree to establish special date nights.**

Set the time, perhaps, Friday night, to go out to dinner, a movie, a walk in the park, or other activities that you both enjoy. Hold this time sacred and make it one of your highest priorities.

Establishing and continuing a *date night* comes rather easily for a newly married couple. Then comes pregnancy and the first child. The tendency is to stay at home with the child, to forget date night. Don't let that happen. The greatest gift parents can give their children is to hold their marriage sacred to the extent that children see and feel their love for each other.

Bride/Wife's Response:

_____
_____
_____
_____
_____
_____
_____
_____

Groom/Husband's Response:

_____
_____
_____
_____
_____
_____
_____
_____

Negotiations/Decision:

_____
_____
_____
_____
_____
_____
_____
_____

65. **Occasionally—preferably at least every six months—plan a weekend away.**

Every couple, even newlyweds, after six months, need a weekend away together—away from work, family, friends—just the two of them. Sure, it will cost a bit. But such a retreat need not require five-star hotels and restaurants. Perhaps a state park lodge, a bed and breakfast or a camping trip would do the trick.

Bride/Wife's Response:

_____
_____
_____
_____
_____
_____
_____
_____

Groom/Husband's Response:

_____
_____
_____
_____
_____
_____

Negotiations/Decision:

_____
_____
_____
_____
_____
_____

66. **Do not lift phrases from your spouse's conversation and make assumptions regarding intent.**

One of the chief causes of frustration in marriage is one spouse making wild guesses about the other's basic intent, without bothering to ask for clarification. If there is a question to be asked, ask it kindly.

Do not be touchy and irritable. One of the problems in marriage is the tendency of all of us to take our frustrations out on the one who happens to be there. That is usually our spouse.

Bride/Wife's Response:

_____
_____
_____
_____
_____
_____
_____
_____

Groom/Husband's Response:

_____
_____
_____
_____
_____
_____
_____
_____

Negotiations/Decision:

_____
_____
_____
_____
_____
_____
_____
_____

67. **Verbalize your needs and wants clearly.**

Do not expect your partner to read your mind. Openly discuss your feelings concerning physical and emotional desires. Discuss sexual preferences.

Try to establish some private time and space for yourself each day. During the solitude think about what you can do to make your spouse's life better. If both do this, what a great life it will be.

Bride/Wife's Response:

_____
_____
_____
_____
_____
_____
_____
_____

Groom/Husband's Response:

_____
_____
_____
_____
_____
_____
_____
_____

Negotiations/Decision:

_____
_____
_____
_____
_____
_____
_____
_____

68. **Limit intruders into your marital space.**

Please note topic # 23, concerning sacred space. Once invasion is permitted, even though it is done with the best of intent, the results can be devastating.

Settle your differences, plan and work out your future, just between the two of you. If you need help, seek professional guidance. Avoid intrusion by siblings, parents and friends, regardless of their good intent.

Bride/Wife's Response:

_____
_____
_____
_____
_____
_____
_____
_____

Groom/Husband's Response:

_____
_____
_____
_____
_____
_____
_____

Negotiations/Decision:

_____
_____
_____
_____
_____
_____
_____

69. **Establish a precise method for negotiating differences.**

Give regular attention to *Communication Techniques*, Chapter II. Share your deepest feelings honestly, openly and with respect for the feelings of your spouse. When there is a problem, it is often the tendency of one or both of the spouses to simply avoid the subject. The problem will not go away because of the lack of attention. Like an untreated wound, it becomes more irritated. At some point, in an unguarded moment, the problem will again surface. Solve the matter completely through communication with honesty, patience and love.

Bride/Wife's Response:

_____
_____
_____
_____
_____
_____
_____

Groom/Husband's Response:

_____
_____
_____
_____
_____
_____
_____

Negotiations/Decision:

_____
_____
_____
_____
_____
_____
_____

70. **Finally, and most important, communicate, communicate, communicate**.

In all marriages, there are times of disagreement. Consider that to be a good thing. It gives you an opportunity to express your feelings. Do so openly, honestly and in a kind and considerate manner.

Every day think about the reasons that drew you to love your spouse. Express those feelings.

Congratulations! You are both on your way to a wonderful life. Enjoy every moment of it.

CONCLUSION

MARRIAGES ARE NOT MADE IN HEAVEN

Love songs, movies, and romance novels concerning marriage are often misleading—marriages are not made in heaven, sex will not solve all problems, romantic feelings are not a dependable emotion, and more money may not make things better.

It is important, from the very beginning, to think beyond the wedding. Weddings provide no warranty, no assurance for a solid marriage. Holding your marriage license is exciting, but there are no guarantees.

In our society, there seems to be a license for almost everything. In some communities, bicycles require a license, but the license does not assure safety. Dogs must wear a license on their collar. Without boundaries, they may run away. Businesses must be licensed, but there is no guarantee for success. Perhaps the marriage license may better be compared to the learner's permit prior to receiving a driver's license. It only permits you to begin a legal relationship. Beyond that, it is all up to the couple. You must make it happen. Marriage requires a lot of work, much planning and a great deal of patience and understanding.

Although the cleric may pronounce you are one, that too, can be misleading. Oneness requires singleness of purpose. Common purpose is the result of planning. Planning comes through communication.

I have personally helped many couples find a happy and lasting marriage, using the seventy topics in this *PLANNING YOUR MARRIAGE* guide. Some other couples who were off to a rocky start in their marriage, were able to smooth out the rough spots in their relationship through their use of *Communication Techniques* in Chapter II.

Donna and I, extremely happy in our marriage, use some parts of the Communication Techniques almost every day.

OUR COMMITMENT

Engagement is very exciting
The wedding is wonderful, too;
But our marriage is the most important
As I show my love daily to you.

Stuff will sometimes be helpful,
With money we will pay the bills;
But it's our love that is everlasting
A cure for marital ills.

Some days will bring trouble,
Others will be filled with glee;
Our love will rise above it all
You are most precious to me.

So, this day I reaffirm my love
With honesty beyond emotion;
I pledge my love to you, my dear,
A lifetime of pure devotion.

_____   _____
Bride/Wife   Groom/Husband

_____
Date